Hero of the Play

Hero of the Play

Richard Harrison

Wolsak and Wynn • Toronto

Some of these poems first appeared in *Index, Poetry Canada
Review,* and *Prism International,* and in the anthology *A Discord
of Flags.*

To Lisa Rouleau, Mark Cochrane, Wendy Phillips, Mark Abley, Julie
Bruck, April Bulmer, Nancy Bullis, my friends in the writing
workshops we formed in Montreal and in Toronto, Gary Geddes,
Betsy Struthers, Isabel Henniger, Neile Graham, James Gurley, and
Rob McKay, who saw this work in various stages of completion
and whose readings, discussion and support honed these poems
more than I could have ever done alone, my deepest thanks.

Cover design by Lisa Rouleau and Scott Douglas
Cover art by Scott Douglas
Photograph by Lisa Rouleau
Typeset in Garamond Light by HeYwire Design
Printed in Canada by
The Coach House Printing Company, Toronto.

The publishers and the author gratefully acknowledge support by
The Canada Council and The Ontario Arts Council.

Wolsak and Wynn Publishers Ltd.
Don Mills Post Office Box 316
Don Mills, Ontario, Canada, M3C 2S7

Canadian Cataloguing in Publication Data
Harrison, Richard, 1957-
 Hero of the Play
Poems.
ISBN 0-919897-42-8
I. Title.
PS8565.A77H4 1994   C811'.54   C94-931256-8
PR91993.H37H4 1994

Second Printing

FOR LISA

I touch down like a player returning from a long road trip with the standings still uncertain. You ask me, *How did it go?*

CONTENTS

THE AFRICAN HOCKEY POEMS
1

When the manager of the gallery in the Hôtel
Ivoire sees the flag on my pack, he tells me he
loves my country and he plays hockey on the rink
that lies chilled like a pie in the middle of the hotel
on the equator where leaves rot as they grow and
the air is sweet as apples with their dying. I say
What position? He says *Left Wing.* I say *Like
Bobby Hull.* And Bobby's name makes it: he draws
his hand up and it smiles at the end of his arm:
this is The Shake, the one that begins with the slap
of palm against palm, the one between men
who've found enough between them to confirm
the world for a day and go on. Tomorrow I will
skate on this rink like the pros back home, way
ahead of schedule and nature; I will tell you
I touched the ice and I could be any boy in love.

2

For the photo shoot on the only rink in the Côte
d'Ivoire, I carry a hockey stick from the Canadian
Embassy through the streets of Abidjan, and the stares
of the passersby say no one knows what it is just as
the inland farmers who had never seen the sea stared
at Ulysses with his oar. The old king waited for those
stares, the oar become a butter churn, a plough, the
village speaker's staff when the business of the day
gives way to night. It is time for the story to be told.

REUNION, OR GRIEVING

Taking a small picture of myself, I cut out my face,
paste it over Brett Hull's face in a photo of him
and Bobby at some charity hockey game in
Duluth. I send you this as further proof that I
practiced with Bobby in '76 when I was scouted
by the Jets for goal. Bobby is proud of his son, the
pride coming only now into the light of the arena
where they are perfectly again husband and child
together. Many will say this is cheap, ask where
was he when Brett was growing up waiting for
Bobby to appear in the almost empty stands of
junior. Today I got the news: months ago my place
was vacant at my stepson's wedding. *How could
you?* the face beneath my face moves my mouth
and asks me.

11

MY FAVOURITES (THE NATIONAL GAME)

This one from the summer of '88 when I picked up the
habit of cards and my father called from Victoria,
collecting with me ... *I've got Bobby Hull,* his voice soft,
proud, my father at his best. It's Bobby at his peak as a
Black Hawk rounding the boards in his own end with
the puck for another break-neck rush up ice. Then this
one, Bobby as a Jet, after the divorce, the time he says
he lost his hair before the world. Here his scalp is
stitched through with brass and goals no one counts
except in brackets. This one — Luc Robitaille, *Best left
winger ever born in Quebec.* Marc gave him to me
hidden in a bowl of popcorn, tattered and folded the
way teenagers love and reject the selfsame thing. And
this one you sent me in the mail because you lived in
Regina and I lived here: Brett Hull, poised, intent, waiting
for the pass.

MALE BONDING

Once I loved other sons as though I found my
brother again: the years of their growing muscles
and tanned skin, the evening excursions to the
arcades downtown where our faces were reflected
in the games the way someone standing in the living
room is on TV when it is off. I thought I could never
leave. The traded player says, I cannot go, I belong
here on the shared ice; these are the men I've
learned to skate with, take a pass, shoot, share the
jubilance of the goal. But he goes, and he puts on
another uniform, and he loves his old team from a
great distance, loving like men around their loss.

LOVE AND THE HOCKEY POOL
1. DRAFT DAY

Among the ten of us who sit together and draft
players by name I know only Robert because once
you and he were lovers. Now you are friends: there
he is. I want it to be as if we had known each other
from the days of table hockey when each of us was
complete and right with himself as instinct. When the
games begin, my pick Bourque goes down with a
shoulder, and Ricci, my horse for Rookie of the Year,
the kid from my adopted home town junior team, he
breaks a hand trying to grab a slapshot. Robert calls
me up and leaves a message: *Your team SUCKS!* he
says and laughs and we become close. But when
Messier, his main man, falls to the ice and cannot rise
without his team-mates' help, the iron box of his face
unhinged, *oh no oh no* going through his mind, his leg
curled like a baby's, I feel no 'there-but-for-the-grace,'
only the gain of my own leg on the scoresheet; now
we are closer.

2. TALKING TRADE

I'm trying to trade with Robert whose defence is
weak, who has a couple of big guns and I might get
one. I must keep in mind the men who disappoint
me — even as now I imagine myself seen through
the eyes of the loves I've abandoned — them I will
let go. I nurtured their photographs, smelled the
numbers of each day's ink, my fingers black with
print. I own them by name alone, and for trading,
that alone is enough.

3. THE CONSUMMATION

And when the trading's done, each says I got the better
deal and holds his new man dearer having won the big
talk afternoon of wooing and of lies. When evening
comes, the highlight films replay assists and goals, we
smile or rise with anticipation or delight at scenes
filmed long ago though we know no human face is
waiting there, nor body needs our love.

4. ICE

About the surface. Counting. Hard-edged things.
Like ice and pennies; in the face-off circle, a skate
cuts *R loves L, R loves L.* The beginning of the story
is the theory of jealousy, the game about everything except the goals and assists, the colourful,
public men we pass between us, your name un-
spoken. This is the meaning of victory — a puck
sliding over ice into the bag of cords that holds a
man to his duty — that I should be the one, the
winner, how I come to love him, hate him, the
mirror your love brings to my face.

AFRICAN HOCKEY POEM 3

This is hockey where it has never been written: an
ordinary stick on an African street, my hand on the
shaft, my foot stubbing the butt. I'm walking the way
I walked as a child in the old world of Tony and
Chris and Russell and me playing the sun below the
level of the street. You couldn't see the ball until it
hit. In Hull's hands it was a million-dollar shot, the
birth of the mask, thousands in the stands waiting for
the stick to go up and back and BOOM — *I know!*
calls a man, and he takes the stick from me and
waggles his head from side to side — *shusshh, shusshh*
he says as surely as I do raised on the sound effects
of ice.

THE FEMININE

My plan for a deck of hockey Tarot cards failed
for want of the truly feminine. I could make some
figure a woman in the game; Canada's women's
team is the best in the world, and maybe I could
push the notion until it does not matter, woman or
man — just The Player. But I'd be lying. This is not
why I love the game, or why its symbols work
like runes in my language. This is a game the
women watch, its gentler moments taken in their
image: The Trainer, running to the Fallen Man
Beside the Boards, cradling the face now loose and
looking skyward in his hands, smoothing his hair
with a towel; the Equipment itself, stockings,
girdles, garters. At the time I did not understand
what the woman next to me at a hockey game
was trying to teach when she wondered aloud
whether she would find a better lover in another
woman as the players below us skated the warm-
up, around and around their own side of Centre,
lofting long, lazy Pucks at their Goalie. There is a
Mask on my face, the game divides us. Again I've
come to a profession of love in words I cannot use
for you, with all the women left in the stands
where I demand that you sit and love it all.

THE PRAISE OF MEN

To their faces, it escapes me, words for the praise of men. To a man I admire, to whom I would say, you have real talent and my envy, all that comes out is, *You're good,* and there I remain, fatherly, in charge of words by not saying them. Give me these players whom I will never meet to hoot and holler out my deepest riskless love that finds no softer words, no shame or venture, merely a game, the bargain sealed with a seat in the blues, my naked face a dab of camouflage, hiding my praise in the open.

FIRST ROUND PICK: PAUL COFFEY

Because two years ago he skated around an entire
team, was stopped at the last minute and collapsed
into Mario's arms, his exhausted face somehow at
peace in failure, knowing those arms; because we
capped him at a hundred points in the pool; he was
the only defenceman taken in the first round;
because he was traded from the first team he
helped to win the Stanley Cup and his coach's good-
bye was, You'll never win again; his description of
himself as a wind-up skater is in *The Hockey Phrase
Book*; because he is constantly one behind the
greatest stars, feeding them the puck; because his
nose is my father's, his look intense as I remember
my father running the day I finally passed him,
running my hardest.

21

DEFENCE MECHANISMS

Because his jaw was broken when he knelt between the shooter and the open net, he's vanished from the line-up. Then the commentators say the team is better without him, and my anger rises: he carried that team all year and now he's gone. Yet I say the same thing about the family I made and left. We are talking these days about children, and the bad example I set when I cut an apple holding it in my palm, and at last, cut my finger. Because I take my hands from my pockets when I see a mother carry her newborn across the threshold of the subway door in case the baby falls, or the doors begin to close. Because once I had four names to offer with my own and now I say they are better off without me.

FOGARTY

Tell me to fuck off, you'd be right; I know nothing
of what it's like to be the most celebrated defenceman in junior, to roll under your skates the recorded
legacy of Bobby Orr, to be photographed with my
stick *on fire* I was that hot at what was it 18? 19? I
can't remember, to become the rushing defenceman
stepfather of four kids and just out of school straight
A's wanting and wanting so much to be a man,
anchor the rush on the sloppiest defence of the
weakest team in the League you love them they are
yours. The shots pour by anyway. All year I wrote
home I was happy, I said, so glad to be chosen. I
almost do not know what's left that's true. I couldn't
answer even the most basic question, When did you
know you were a defenceman? I mean, you must
have believed in yourself when no one else did, and
now you want to be anywhere but there, taking the
face off in the middle of the ring of a drink poured
carelessly, spilled over ice.

23

AFRICAN HOCKEY POEM 4: YAMOUSSOUKRO

On the bus to Yamoussoukro the video is Kung Fu and
guns. We are driven past the rainforest, its fierce green
race against dying on the limb. If we had silence the
forest would seem lazy and calm in the humid morning,
leaves drooping like hounds, wind in the long leaves
like someone at the other end of the rink sliding to a
halt, spraying the snow. I saw Gordie Howe flick a stick
full of rinkchaff over the head of a guy looking for
autographed pucks at an Old-Timers game, Gordie
sending the snow in a perfect arc from the blade resting
on the ice. Even the guy had to admire his dexterity, a
lifetime of moving the body just so. So he said *thank-
you.* My friend in the Abidjan street would have
admired Gordie's joke. He handed me back my stick and
laughed. Around us the youngest sons of the Ivory
Coast practised their national game with an egg-shaped
ball paprika-red with dust. On the other side of town
their country's team was showing the world how to
kick and the stadium was singing 60,000 strong. But
days and miles away from the city, the soundtrack on
the bus is someone hitting someone with a bag of
broken glass; outside becomes the jungle of my father's
war that I see in the way he walks through a clearing in
the trees: cannonfire in the verdant air. And I feel the
pull of my father's will for home, the years that bound
our troubled house like wheat by wire so that nothing
could escape to this wind.

ALL-STAR ACTION

*— January 19, 1991: Desert Storm begins the war on
Iraq 3 days before the Annual All-Star Game*

Even the greatest player in the world asks *What
are we here for?* and votes to cancel play. But
they don't, just as I am writing this, when the war
has begun, and bombs become the Thousand
Points of Light once the bad joke of an American
election. The men shift listlessly on their skates as
a woman whose brother is a pilot in the Gulf sings
the National Anthem. The puck is dropped. Later I
will scan the papers for the numbers that mean the
acts of men. And as they score the surface, we
hear again the scour of metal on ice; the crowd
stares past them, dizzy with fear for the boys they
are so proud of. Below the ice, distant at first, and
moving under the sliding men, they appear: blade-
shaped, graphic the way insects are, the airplanes.
They rise towards the ice from the sky below,
larger now, faster, their steel tails scraping the ice;
they move under the men, imitating them perfectly
— passing, shooting . . . passing, shooting.

FACE-OFF

They lean forward, sticks extended, faces poised almost,
from my angle, as if to kiss as they kissed in the NBA
Finals: Isiah Thomas and Magic Johnson: the name of
a prophet, the faith of a wizard. Can we hope for such
reconciliation? Hallowe'en at last a memorial for 300
years of women burning for their knowledge at the
pyres of the Church, men, crowded around their good
good work, their faces implacable even with the
screaming in their ears; for men to kiss while thousands
cheer them, or is it only here, the imagined ground,
where faces are not masks, are not brought bare into
each other's view only to dare each other — take this off
if you can.

ALL-TIME GAME

One on one we are drafting the all-time game
between us my brother and I, not the Official All-
Time Team of Six with no one to play; we are truly
opposed, the language inflated and gross the way
men talk when they mean it pretending they don't.
The Big Six are all English which I say reflects the
voters. Then I say I could beat those guys with
Lemieux, Robitaille, Richard up front; Bourque &
Savard at the blueline. Plante in net. He says we
should draft for the ultimate game, and the heavy
checkers come out of our mouths, the *policemen*,
and our finesse players get banged up along the
boards. The game deteriorates; because he nearly
killed a man, I pick Eddie Shore. It's like this over
table hockey, us at each other, huge pucks in the
tiny nets, the anger of 30 years, everything out of
proportion.

COACH'S CORNER

The almost clerical collar, he is the priest of rock 'em
sock 'em. He silences his more knowledgeable friends
with his faith in the bodies of men and without him
and his kind the NHL would be vapid as the All-Star
Game forever. He is loud and whiny and complaining
and chokes up on air if he's hurt by someone's words —
everything a man should not be, yet every sports bar
wills itself to quiet, turns up the volume on its dozen
sets only for his words. He is their man in a way no
hero of the play could be; his big league career was a
single game, but remember, he used to tell Bobby Orr
what to do and Bobby listened as we listen though we
let the game go on in silence. He slams foreigners,
praises women in all the ways wrong for our time,
rejects any wavering in the masculinity of his troops
like a colonel in the US Marines. And yet he is here
because he is unafraid to love, love the game, the
journeyman players, love the code that makes a man a
man and if you don't know, I ain't gonna tell ya. He
loves the fans, for all the pain they cause him, and we
are here with our own uncomfortable backs for that
dogged love, the voice that rises like a tenor sax,
pointed fingers, eyes narrowed to see clear and deep
the world that has him trapped on two sides already.

USING THE BODY

It's the instruction for goons, use the body, pound
the other guy rougher than his game imagines, the
body hitting home, the body the agent of policy.
When a fight begins, we say it is emotion, but after
the game, the goon speaks clearly of motive, the
momentum of play, doing what he has to do, a strict
account level in his head. Later, when he wears a
suit, when he coaches, you can see how he saw the
entire rink all along: he never looked at the puck,
the stickwork, a man's cheek when his purpose is
clear and there's open ice before him. He saw the
solid mass of a man, how the game, flimsy as a
wing, could be held at the socket where the wing
joins the body, and broken.

THE USE OF FORCE

— New York Rangers at Montreal, February 9, 1991

It boils at the centre of the game: Lyle, the home team
boy, pulling Randy, from New York, away from the
clot of men in the corner of the rink. Lyle wants to
fight, and Randy, the smaller man, holds Lyle's jersey
at the cuffs, trying to pin his arms. Gently, almost like
leaves on a stream, they drift towards Centre, their
hands naked now, their heads unhelmeted; this is the
undressing. Soon we'll see them pull at each other's
sweaters, we'll see the padding each man has strapped
around his chest, the body covered in fragments: a
piece . . . a space . . . a piece . . . . But then big Lyle's hand
pops free and his bared fist goes down and down on
Randy's face, and the crowd's anticipation, the listless,
frustrating play of the home team, bursts from the
throats of the 17000 at the Forum that night, a roar I
can feel tremble down the centre of my ribcage, my
stomach, my groin, the way Polynesian sailors without
compasses navigated their reedy boats, their genitals
feeling the roll of the sea (and I'm in Canada in a huge,
cold room). Lyle has finished his offering to the crowd,
and the officials draw lines between him and the
shaking Randy; I can still hear my parents saying, when
I saw my first hockey fight on TV, *They can't punch
very hard on skates.* But Randy has been brought to
the ice, his sky filled with Lyle's fist, and the Rangers
do not fare well this night, while the Canadiens find
Caesar's tide, and break the game open in their favour.

I WATCH HIM BREAK SANDSTROM'S LEG

and I find myself longing for a big, tough man
with a nickname like *The Hammer* as if an enforcer
with the right rink smarts and the will to go the
distance with anyone on the ice could protect his
friends from the kind of hit that ends a career, the
violence within the rules. Fact is, there is no fight;
fact is the Kings go down in six. We've just been
through a war — even that is not enough when men
are willing, the outcome is in doubt and the ache in
me is to strike, I who am not hungry, not broken.

LINDROS

has become unavoidable, appears in the *NHL 75th Anniversary Commemorative Book* though at the time of printing he hadn't played a minute for an NHL team; some people make your history from the outside like Marx and Russia where they played the team concept to perfection. When their veterans came over the skill they lacked most was taking the shot without passing, and Makarov led the League without scoring a goal. Ken Dryden says the famous *soft hands* is because the Russians were afraid of breaking their shoddy sticks, but Lindros is afraid of breaking nothing. I saw him bust a man's collarbone in Maple Leaf Gardens and nearly break another man's leg, score one goal and assist on another. The fans went wild, and it proves how little we have for ourselves: given the chance, I'd be him and you are right to doubt my love.

RUSSIANS

We need them. They made the act of a single Canadian
Canada's act in '72, the shot so sweet it has replayed a
million times: Henderson, leaping, faces the camera as if
to each of us; Cournoyer embraces his ribs, the word
Canada on his shoulders. And the Soviets, confused,
upset, they left him uncovered and Canada's greatest
shot was a rebound; I tell you how it felt to win, and
you, trying to love me in this moment, ask, *Who's this?*
Tretiak, their goalie a crab on its back every limb
kicking out to stop what's already been done. *And this?*
Number 25 on the Russian defence — *I don't know,* his
name unwritten below the painting of this photograph
in the Hall of Fame, and on the back of the Summit
Series Anniversary card where he takes up a quarter of
the frame and already he understands what they've lost.
They played the better game and should have beaten
the high-priced men who laughed at their ancient skates
and the way the trainer collected the pucks in a bucket
during practice because they had so few. He sees himself as a promising child; he made the older boys look
clumsy in their parents' eyes and the words *National
Team* were said in his presence and he never saw those
boys again; he sees his junior team beating yet another
country, the fans sullen and quiet in the stands round
home ice; he sees the young man whose leg was broken
during tryouts and never healed right. They turn to face
him. Player by player he sees the death of his league,
and in the distance he sees Phil Esposito with his own
team in the NHL take the podium on draft day and
with all the world to choose from pluck a kid from
Europe happy to make it on the only rinks that count.
He did his job; they almost won; his own name forgotten, he is looking where you are and you are asking me,
find him.

33

THE SWEATER

Could I tell you he was beautiful, returned from
winter camp in a sweater really from the team whose
crest it bore, him standing among us with our hands
outstretched; I touched the cloth. Shall I tell you of his
smile, his reckless arms that day; in a hockey town he
was a son in his father's own colours, how the son
once called his favourite teacher *coach* and the father,
meeting that teacher, took his thin, long hand in his
huge fingers, enfolding it in inescapable size and said
my son loved you! Shall I speak of love then, too? a
black suit burning gold at the edge; in the middle of
class this young man held up his arm in a sleeve of
Stanley Cups.

PENALTY

This was the day Nelson Mandela came to say
thank-you to West Africa, the day Nelson and the
dictator of Ghana were driven though the city
streets in an open truck. A people's day, the way
cleared by troops looking for assassins, seeing them
everywhere — Mandela was coming! The crowd I
was in surged forward, breaking the plane of the
curb like a goal line. The soldiers stopped. The
crowd booed. And a certain soldier got out of his
jeep, glaring. A woman whispered *leave,* but I stood
the way a fan stands at the glass for the action on
the other side. And down came his boot all the way
from the Second World War, and the crowd spun
round, pivoting in their sandals, and ran and
knocked me down so I lay in the street with all
their sandals like the gloves on the ice after a bench
brawl.

AT THE HOCKEY HALL OF FAME I SAW

the Russian sweaters from '72: they were homemade
and eccentric — wool with tiny, felt letters sewn on,
the letters curled from the wool, like the bits on the
costumes my mother sewed for the school Centennial
show where I played a boy transported 100 years into
the future, to the Canada I'd never see: smooth-running
and prosperous and completely English. Like the
school. Above their old clothes, the players move in
ways only skating can offer: hips extended, heads
leaning, the arms forging a perfect circuit with the stick
and the padded shoulders, legs together to the side, an
angle only speed delivers from falling.

Because they make decisions while moving, they are
not stunned by the terrible moment the puck hits
the stick, the skaters swirling like oil; in that moment,
they are perfect and faster than the speed of our
judgement. Only later does a man weep for his dead
father who believed for so long in his son. Only later
does it return to mind that management has cheated
him, or tomorrow he might be traded, or injured, or
wake in a city he does not love without a father to
call in the middle of his night, or somehow it might
leave him, what he is just before he glances up and
shoots,
with only papers before him and no steel on his feet.

THE SILENCE OF 17000

— Montreal Forum, December 11, 1989

17000 who came for noise drawn to silence in their
memory this building the shape of the inside of the
mouth it waits for air the women of L'Ecole
Polytechnique fill the Forum we swear we will never
forget but words return and we take sides dressed in
language as the men we surround are dressed in
opposing cities we shame and glorify ourselves each
season the enemy goalie wears a white ribbon under
his helmet he shakes his head when the siren sounds
the game begins the police arrive too late: as many
dead as on the ice before us.

SHRINE

Surrounded by the dead, the cool stone walls of the
dead, the stain of glass backlit by the African sun
blazing with the faces of the vividly departed —
Age 31; Age 34, the age at which now, here, a man
hangs up his skates and goes into business or
coaching. On the cards, the high speed film traps
Béliveau and Hull mid-flight. When a generation's
work is done by 35, by the time you're 35, you've
seen four generations. I remember Keon and
Armstrong of the last great Leafs; Espo and Orr and
Boston; I remember Lafleur and I remember the
Islanders. I remember Gretzky entering the game.
Imagine a life the span a career is now, how it must
be to grow old, polish the names you knew as a
child so they would not be forgotten the way
names are forgotten to all but collectors of plaques
and cards, the names entwined in their absence
with love.

STANLEY CUP

At the centre of the circle of the Champions of the
World, Mario Lemieux hoists the Cup, kisses its silver
thigh, the names of men where *his* will soon be cut
with a finish pure as a mirror; around him, the
tumult. And Scotty Bowman, the winningest coach
in the NHL, named his first son Stanley when his
Canadiens won it in '73 with a stonewall blueline and
a dizzying transition game. Every player on every
team who ever won the Cup gets to take it home; it
has partied on front lawns, swimming pools and in
the trunks of cars, and even the man who left it on
the side of the road and drove away, still he thinks
of it as holy. And that word — holy — appears most
in the conversation of veterans who know how the
touch fades, the shoulder takes longer between days
of easy movement, how Bobby Hull passed over his
chance to drink champagne from its lip when the
Hawks won it '61 because he thought there'd be so
many in his life. Some take the Cup apart, clean the
rings, make minor repairs in their basements, and
then inscribe on the inside of the column the un-
official log of their intimate knowledge: This way
I have loved you.

LANGUAGE

This is the season Jagr will blossom: his 3rd as a pro,
2 Stanley Cups, a great playoffs behind him. This year
John Kordic is dead; in my mind I've followed him after
games to the strip bars of Yonge Street where John
bought the line that sex can be made as simple as
hockey; in the dark of the Zanzibar he finds his place
smoothly, opens the hands he balled into fists in the
Gardens; he calls a woman to his table to dance; before
she begins, he says *Don't turn around.* In the pool, we
are gearing up for the draft, the League in flux because
of the European talent. Did you see Jagr score in the
game that eliminated Chicago? stick-handling around
three men then sliding the puck like a surprise confes-
sion under Belfour? They asked him how he did it, but
he couldn't explain; lacking the language to describe his
own body, he is only more beautiful.

JERGUS BACA

My last pick of the '91 season, *a Czechoslovakian
Superstar* said *The Hockey News.* He idolizes Bobby
Orr, wants to play for Hartford, where Bobby
works now; he is given the number 4, Bobby's
number. My surprise on the guys in the pool, he
would storm from the defensive zone, catch my
friends blindside (*How did you* know *this guy?*) as
he takes the game in his superstar hands, the way
Bobby played the opposition and his own men like
two sides of table hockey in his time. I saw his
maiden shift in Maple Leaf Gardens, my voice
alone with his name.

OPEN TO THE PUBLIC

— Visitors' Dressing Room, Maple Leaf Gardens. (To usher in a new era, in the autumn of 1992, management invited fans to tour the building freely for the first time in years.)

Most teams spent the '70s and '80s in here holding the
lead on the Leafs, this tiny room with the missing
hooks replaced by 3 inch nails haphazard from the
walls as if they'd grown; the guy behind me on our
tour inhales it deeply through his nose, throws out his
arms to get even more of the sweaty air into his lungs
the way you'd hold a filling wineskin by the corners ...
It's a locker room all right! he exhales loud and happy
and 17; it's the room at school where he and his team
work out together and for the Yearbook photograph
gathered naked behind the weights; they'll laugh about
it when it's printed, and years from now ask *where's
that guy? and him? and him? whatever happened?*
the way men who played for those Leafs look hard at
team pictures for what they might have been had they
only visited this place they spent their short careers as
pro; with a stadium so empty it filled 4 pages in *Sports
Illustrated,* the fans in Minnesota shamed their team's
lousy owners from the rink. Toronto booed Bobby Orr
with sell-out crowds and hung his sweater on a nail.

43

MEMENTO

— March, 1992, the first full-scale strike in League history

See these tickets? greys for the first game not
played because of the strike, the one against the
Islanders who skated on Garden ice that afternoon
then turned in their skates, and the team locked
their colours away as if they'd died. This was the
game they were going to raise Ace Bailey's jersey to
the rafters, high over his beloved ice, so he could
see that memory had not died, and the hanging
cloth would fill with cheers like a chest. Ace
suffered a stroke instead, the Gardens emptied by
the strike. There are many kinds of silence. The
team is gone, but I support the players in this game.
At the negotiating table, my own mouth has filled
with the crabapple taste of talk unheard because
we could not strike. Among the protesting fans last
night demanding the performance of the game, and
knowing he might be on TV, a man in his team's
colours wears a ballcap with two pink cloth breasts
icing the peak. Ace nearly died on Garden ice: in
1933, Eddie Shore, mistaking him for another
member of his team, leapt up from a check and
struck him down from behind; next morning the
papers wrote as if he'd already died. And though
he lived, he never played again. Later, Ace shook
Eddie's hand at Centre Ice; this is how he felt about
the game. Ace died the same day they said the
League itself was finished by the strike; I've packed
away my hockey sweater, though I love the game
and I love my brother who gave me the colours of
the team: I collect their signs like the kind of love

44

poem written only with the eyes — not about love, but
what you'd do if you had the chance: the players
speak of icing their own teams, and the owners
threaten replacement players as their ace in the hole.
But everyone's still talking despite the strike, so let's say
they're going to ice the playoffs after all. The game
goes on, and hope has not yet died; let's say these
tickets are good: at some game after the strike, this tit-
headed guy would sit down beside me, turn his face
from the ice and say, *I love this team.* I'd know what
he meant. I'd disagree.

HIS FATHER'S NUMBER
Version 1

John Cullen on Gardens Ice with his father's
number, better than the flag to wrap an admiring
son; his father in the stands like a patriot, father of
numbers. And the father glows on his son's back in
the light of the stadium. This is hockey's most
treasured story: men grow old under their numbers
which are their names from the lofty seats, and the
day their names come again. In my father's flesh
are memories of the body become manly and
skilled; there is always the test of *true to yourself*,
and a man can see his answer in the way his body
cuts through a chilling air, stretches out his arms
into the sleeves of his father's shirt.

LEMIEUX, AND THE NEWS

is cancer, and the doctors assure us of his strength, the
high probability of health. We say all we care about is
him even if he never plays again though we want him
back on the ice as he was, victorious. The news is the
punishment of Iraq, a surgical strike, the language
confusing life with one of its parts and not by accident
either. Today my friend Bill lost his friend who wore
his white hair long as if the Sixties meant his age,
quoted with a tongue full of English letters, disdained
sentiment and had a collection of shillings, he said,
because of their shape. And this, suddenly, after weeks
of chemo and a good prognosis. Bill visited him the day
before, the way I wish I had visited when I had the
chance: do the usual talk about a book, eat and drink
all evening, laughing at what they expect you to
believe night after night, saying *See you tomorrow* like
it was the most normal thing in the world.

ON THE AMERICAN EXPRESS AD PHOTO OF CARDMEMBERS GORDIE HOWE AND WAYNE GRETZKY TALKING AFTER THE GAME

The old man holds his hands in the middle air
before him, raised and loose, explaining something
only he and the kid who took his place in the record
book even understand as a question. Hockey looks
simple and fast the way Sumo looks simple and fast,
and there are 78 named moves in Sumo though a
match is over in 9 seconds or less, the time it takes
a man to score a goal and the two who get assists to
set him up. Advice is briefly spoken, takes years to
hear; Gordie said to Wayne, *Work on your back-
hand.* Later Gretzky's father will lie dying in a
Hamilton hospital and Wayne will take a check from
behind into the boards. By reflex, he will take off his
helmet, his heavy gloves, undressing himself on the
ice in his pain, his own armour too heavy for his
shocked skin. Unprotected, brought low, he will look
the way he doesn't think he looks here, in this photo,
receiving Gordie's wisdom, the weight of the game
flooding his limbs beyond bearing.

ACTS OF WORSHIP

*If you're too much in awe, you'll never love this
game. Sooner or later, you've got to hit Gordie and
flatten him if you can the way Henry Moore used to
have his kids piss on each of his sculptures when
they were done to show they were, after all, only
things. Of course you can't. Gordie is just too strong.
But if you're lucky he'll give you an elbow behind
the ref's back and you'll see what a bastard he is.
That'll cure you.*

AUTOGRAPH

The first day in the market town of Abidjan I was
touched by a thousand hands, the bead sellers and
sellers of hats, a man holding a statue, a man with
two masks, a woman selling silver and dyed cloth
dazzling in the emergent sun. Ten thousand
touches I cannot bear, and voices calling out.
Without billboards or the cool face of TV this is
business: to touch, to call. The intrusions back
home are privacy to me now, the way I am alone
as I walk the selling streets; here, I dream of birds,
here I write to you I never knew what it was like
to be whistled at in the streets, approached for sex
like it was something you could take from your
pocket. This is your face on my body, the face of
stars besieged by autograph well-wishers, *give me
something of your body in motion, your success,
something I do not have. I'll give you a good deal,*
birds in a flurry of corn thrown over water,
I love you! give me your name.

RHEAUME

Here is the desire of Manon Rhéaume: to stop the
puck. Come down from the stands, strap on the big
pads, painted mask, disappear into *goalie* the way
a man can be a man and not a man inside the
armour. To forget in the motion of the save that we
do not forget she is always a woman and sex is
everything: if she wasn't pretty she'd never hear her
looks got her on the NHL team in Tampa Bay
where the ushers are women hired from a bar
called *Hooters*, and David Letterman wouldn't have
her on *Late Night* prodding her again and again, *Say
Ock-ee*; if Brett Hull was ugly as a wet owl and
scored 86 goals a season, still there'd be kids with
his poster on their bedroom doors. To be a woman
and have it be her play that counts. To stop the
puck where the best are men, for men to be better
than they are. On your wall is a collage of women
with their arms raised, they are dancing, they are
lifting weights, they are marching against apartheid.
One is a goddess with snakes in her hands;
Catwoman reaches for Gotham, Boadicea shakes a
spear in the face of Rome, two nuns run splashing
into the laughing waves: here, I give you Rhéaume
and a glove save, the puck heading for the top
corner. Stopped.

WITHOUT WORDS

— In October, 1992, Calgary centre Joe Nieuwendyk was elbowed in the throat and suffered an injury to his larynx. At the time it was feared he'd never speak again.

I speak as a shell speaks, remembering in the cavern of its heart the roaring ocean that tossed it up to a human hand. Turn your face from the Saddledome on a Saturday night. There I am pure action, and innocent as hockey itself when winter stuns the mouth of the river and metal chafes ice into boys at play, their words only half a language and loved for that. Like poetry. I approach. My whole body becomes the lump in my throat as if his charging elbow is still there, as if it will last forever, as if the iced and wasted land ended in a bang along the boards one night. But I have our names within me, close my lips around the roughened air, and the world begins again between us in a whisper.

THE GREATS

These are the figures of my escapes: men who could
fly, bend steel, come to life each month in my eager
eyes, my flight from my father's face. Determined men
I watch cross and re-cross the comic-panel lines that
mark their play; these are my figures, the Greats.
A sheet of ice puts a man in motion at impossible
angles for the physics of the shoe; an ink-filled brush
over thick paper . . . *I can move like you.*

MY FATHER'S FACE

To begin (always beginning) to speak of my father's
face uncovered at last — Coffey's determined look
up ice, Messier's gaze which weighs 200 pounds, the
faces of the village elders of Ghana who are their
world's law and I stared into through a camera
which is my only permission to look so long; I look
away and down; the eyes of the player captured on
film beating another for the sports page, a red glove
breaks a jaw (the man plays with emotion); my
father as a boy, his face in a grip between the thumb
and index of his father's hand, my grandfather
saying, *A small face, as big as a two-penny ball,* my
father disgraced by a story years old; he picks a
squash ball up and it reminds him, the words work
his jaw like his favourite poems, the language
excessive with meaning; there, within the eyes of the
soldier who made the crowd round me run from his
stamped foot so fast they left their shoes in the
street, the face that could shoot; that face, advancing
on me over that fight at dinner: for backing down
from that face myself I have praised and been
praised for the peace; I have made so much peace
backing down; shot along the boards of a perfect
rink, the puck describes the universe and returns,
that face I show you in anger my own.

HIS FATHER'S NUMBER
Version 3

John Cullen on Gardens Ice, his father's number, my
father's mouth trembling and wet waiting again as I
have waited too long between the last word and the
next; the crowd pauses.

Hello, Dad. This is my hockey. Did you ever see me play it? I dream you in the stands, no longer running. You appear in my words as if years ago you died and made absence your only fault. This is the lie that keeps us looking in the faces of worshipped men: if only you were there, then everything would have been OK, everything would have been good. Really, you are perfect, perfect in the fearful story, perfect in the highlight film, perfect as you limp from the ice between your team-mates, the iron box of your face unhinged *oh no oh no* going through your mind as you cannot put your weight down; you are perfect in your demonstration of the triple jump that won you the Championship of the army games in Asia; perfect again in your every word your son is not a strong boy, your allergic son who breathes whistling in the sick spring air.

RICCI

In your first game for Philadelphia you, a centre,
reached out at your own blueline and tried to catch a
slapshot. You broke your hand, lost your chance at
Rookie of the Year; where you played junior I made
a stepfamily. You woke up this morning traded, the
clock at zero; the bones in your hand ache: at my
wedding there will be no stepsons, -daughter; there
will be Lisa and me, and this time I will give my
whole body, even the bones that once were broken.

HUSH

ssshhhh, sshhhh, the skater stops, *Husshhhh,* turning
his body sideways to the flow of his body, the ice.
Hush, my beloved son, in whom I am well pleased;
this painful land smiles inside the leper in the
street; her extended hand — you take it, *sshhhh,* no
one is here who has ever done you harm, no one;
you might die in this land which is to say, you
might die here and the strange place makes what
you have always known clear to you — *what
would you have left undone?* The sound of ice,
the puck cradled in the stick, the skater turns *sshhh,*
the bath is drawn, warm water, my huge hand;
you have found me out.

Richard Harrison's first two books are *Fathers Never Leave You* and *Recovering the Naked Man*. He has degrees in biology and philosophy from Trent University, and an M.A. in English from Concordia. Currently he is a full-time writer, editor, and hockey fan in Toronto.